William Robinson

Garden Design and Architects' Gardens

Two Reviews, Illustrated, to Show, by Actual Examples from British Gardens...

William Robinson

Garden Design and Architects' Gardens

Two Reviews, Illustrated, to Show, by Actual Examples from British Gardens...

ISBN/EAN: 9783337049362

Printed in Europe, USA, Canada, Australia, Japan

Cover: Foto ©Lupo / pixelio.de

More available books at **www.hansebooks.com**

BY THE SAME

ALPINE FLOWERS for English Gardens. Second Edition.

THE SUB-TROPICAL GARDEN; or, Beauty of Form in the Flower Garden. Second Edition.

HARDY FLOWERS. Description of upwards of 1300 of the most ornamental species, with Directions for their Arrangement, Culture, etc. Fourth and Cheaper Edition.

THE WILD GARDEN; or, Our Graves and Gardens made beautiful by the Naturalisation of Hardy Exotic Plants. Illustrated by ALFRED PARSONS. Second Edition. John Murray.

THE ENGLISH FLOWER GARDEN: Style, Position, and Arrangement. Followed by a Description of all the best Plants for it—their Culture and Arrangement. Second Edition, 1889. John Murray.

GOD'S ACRE BEAUTIFUL; or, The Cemeteries of the Future. Third Edition. With Illustrations. London: John Murray. New York: Scribner & Welford. Published in a cheaper form and with additions under the name—

CREMATION AND URN-BURIAL. Cassell & Co., Limited.

THE PARKS AND GARDENS OF PARIS. Considered in Relation to the Wants of other Cities, and of Public and Private Gardens. Being notes made in Paris Gardens. Third Edition. Illustrated. London: John Murray.

JOURNALS

THE GARDEN. An Illustrated Weekly Journal of Gardening in all its branches. Vol. XL.

GARDENING ILLUSTRATED. For Town and Country. A Weekly Journal for Amateurs and Gardeners. Vol XIII.

FARM AND HOME. A Weekly Illustrated Journal of Agriculture in all its branches. Stock, Dairy, Tillage, Stable, Pasture, Orchard, Market-Garden, Poultry, House. Vol. X.

WOODS AND FORESTS. A Weekly Illustrated Journal of Forestry, Ornamental Planting, and Estate Management. Vols. I. and II. 1885.

GARDEN DESIGN

AND ARCHITECTS' GARDENS

Two reviews, illustrated, to show, by actual examples from British gardens, that clipping and aligning trees to make them 'harmonise' with architecture is barbarous, needless, and inartistic

by

W. Robinson, F.L.S.

London :
John Murray, Albemarle Street
1892

PREFACE

> That we might see eyes were given us; and a tongue to tell accurately what we had got to see. It is the alpha and omega of all intellect that man has. No poetry, hardly even that of Goethe, is equal to the true image of reality—had one eyes to see that.—T. CARLYLE, *Letters to Varnhagen Von Ense.*

The one English thing that has touched the heart of the world is the English garden. Proof of this we have in such noble gardens as the English park at Munich, the garden of the Emperor of Austria at Laxenberg, the Petit Trianon at Versailles, the parks formed of recent years round Paris, and many lovely gardens in Europe and America. The good sense

*of English writers and landscape gardeners
refused to accept as right or reasonable the
architect's garden, a thing set out as bricks
and stones are, and the very trees of which
were mutilated to meet his views as to
" design," or rather to prove his not being
able to see the simplest elements of design
in landscape beauty or natural form. And
some way or other they destroyed nearly
all signs of it throughout our land.*

*In every country where gardens are made
we see the idea of the English garden grate-
fully accepted; and though there are as yet
no effective means of teaching the true art
of landscape gardening, we see many good
results in Europe and America. No good
means have ever been devised for the teaching of this delightful English art. Here
and there a man of keen sympathy with
Nature does good work, but often it is
carried out by men trained for a very
different life, as engineers in the great*

Paris parks, and in our own country by surveyors and others whose training often wholly unfits them for the study of the elements of beautiful landscape. Thus we do not often see good examples of picturesque garden and park design, while bad work is common. Everywhere—unhappily, even in England, the home of landscape gardening—the too frequent presence of stupid work in landscape gardening offers some excuse for the two reactionary books which have lately appeared—books not worth notice for their own sake, as they contribute nothing to our knowledge of the beautiful art of gardening or garden design. But so many people suppose that artistic matters are mere questions of windy argument, that I think it well to show by English gardens and country seats of to-day that the many sweeping statements of their authors may be disproved by reference to actual things, to be seen by all who care for them. We live at a time when, through complexity of thought and speech, artistic questions have got into a maze of confusion. Even teachers by profession confuse themselves and their unfortunate pupils with vague and hyper-refined talk about art and "schools" and "styles," while all the time much worse work is done than in days when simpler, clearer views were held. To prove this there is the example of the great Master's work and the eternal laws of nature, on the study of which all serious art must be for ever based. Beneath all art there are laws, however subtle, that cannot be ignored without error and waste; and in garden design there are lessons innumerable both in wild and cultivated Nature which will guide us well if we seek to understand them simply.

These books are made up in great part of quotations from old books on gardening—many of them written by men who knew books better than gardens. Where the authors touch the ground of actuality, they soon show little acquaintance with the subject; and, indeed, they see no design at all in landscape gardening and admit their ignorance of it. That men should write on things of which they have thought little is unhappily of frequent occurrence, but to find them openly avowing their ignorance of the art they presume to criticise is new.

A word or two on the state of architecture itself may not be amiss. From Gower Street to the new Law Courts our architecture does not seem to be in a much better state than landscape gardening is, according to the architects to whom we owe the " Formal Garden" and " Garden Craft" ! It is William Morris—whose " design" these authors may respect — who calls London houses " mean and idiotic rabbit warrens:" so that there is plenty to do for ambitious young architects to set their own house in artistic order!

As regards "formal gardening," the state of some of the best old houses in England — Longleat, Compton-Wynyates, Brympton, and many others, where trees in formal lines, clipped or otherwise, are not seen in connection with the architecture — is proof against the need of the practice. As regards the best new houses, Clouds, so well built by Mr. Philip Webb, is not any the worse for its picturesque surroundings, which do not meet the architect's senseless craving for "order and balance"; while Batsford, certainly one of the few really good new houses in England, is not disfigured by the fashions in formality the authors wish to see revived, and of which they give an absurd example in a cut of Badminton. There is, in short, ample proof, furnished both by the beautiful old houses of England and by those new ones that have any claim to dignity, that the system they seek to revive could only bring costly ugliness to our beautiful home-landscapes.

W. R.

July 1, 1892.

CONTENTS

	PAGE
Garden Design . .	1
Natural and False Lines .	5
"Uncultivated Nature" .	8
The True Landscape .	13
Buildings in Relation to the Garden	16
Time and Gardens	20
True Use of a Garden	23
Formal Gardening	25
"Nature," and what we mean by it .	31
"All Our Paths" are Crooked !	35
"The Only Garden Possible !"	40
"No Design in Landscape"	43
No Grass in Landscape Gardening ! .	46
"Improving" Battersea Park ! .	50
Nature and Clipped Yews	53
No Line in Nature !	62
"Vegetable Sculpture"	66

ILLUSTRATIONS

RHIANVA .	*To face page*	2
GROUP OF TREES ON GARDEN LAWN AT GOLDER'S HILL, HAMPSTEAD	*Page*	4
WAKEHURST . .	*To face page*	6
GILBERT WHITE'S HOUSE AT SELBORNE	,,	10
EXAMPLE OF FORMAL GARDENING	*Page*	12
LONGLEAT . . .	*To face page*	16
OLD PLACE, LINDFIELD	,,	18
ARUNDEL CASTLE .	,,	20
TAILPIECE .	*Page*	22
WEST DEAN . .	*To face page*	24
ATHELHAMPTON HALL, DORSET	,,	26
THE VICARAGE GARDEN, ODIHAM	,,	30
UNCLIPPED TREES AT THE LITTLE TRIANON	*Page*	34
WESTONBIRT .	*To face page*	36
THRUMPTON HALL	,,	40

b

ILLUSTRATIONS

Tailpiece	*Page* 45
Goodwood .	*To face page* 46
Avenue in Paris	,, 50
Clipped Trees at the Little Trianon	*Page* 52
The "Grange," Hartley Wintney .	*To face page* 54
A Yew Tree on Mountain, N. England	,, 56
Building in Paris	,, 58
Broadlands, Hants .	,, 64
Warren House, Coombe Wood	,, 66
Drummond Castle .	,, 68
Madresfield	,, 70
Tailpiece .	*Page* 73

"*The number of those who really think seriously before they begin to write is small; extremely few of them think about the subject itself; the remainder think only about the books that have been written on it.*"—ARTHUR SCHOPEN-
HAUER.

GARDEN DESIGN[1]

A BEAUTIFUL house in a fair landscape is the most delightful scene of the cultivated earth—all the more so if there be an artistic garden—the rarest thing to find! The union—a happy marriage it should be—between the house beautiful and the ground near it is worthy of more thought than it has had in the past, and the best ways of effecting that union artistically should interest men more and more as our cities grow larger and our lovely English landscape shrinks

[1] *The Formal Garden in England.* By Reginald Blomfield and F. Inigo Thomas. London : Macmillan and Co.

B

back from them. The views of old writers will help us little, for a wholly different state of things has arisen in these mechanical days. My own view is that we have never yet got from the garden, and, above all, the home landscape, half the beauty which we may get by abolishing the needless formality and geometry which disfigure so many gardens, both as regards plan and flower planting. Formality is often essential in the plan of a flower garden near a house—*never* as regards the arrangements of its flowers or shrubs. To array these in lines or rings or patterns can only be ugly wherever done!

That men have never yet generally enjoyed the beauty that good garden design may give is clear from the fact that the painter is driven from the garden! The artist dislikes the common garden with its formality and bedding; he cannot help hating it! In a country

Rhianva. Terraced garden, but with picturesque planting and flower gardening.

place he will seek anything but the garden, but may, perhaps, be found near a wild Rose tossing over the pigsty. This dislike is natural and right, as from most flower gardens the possibility of any beautiful result is shut out! Yet the beautiful garden exists, and there are numbers of cottage gardens in Surrey or Kent that are as " paintable " as any bit of pure landscape!

Why is the cottage garden often a picture, and the gentleman's garden near, wholly shut out of the realm of art, a thing which an artist cannot look at long? It is the absence of pretentious " plan " in the cottage garden which lets the flowers tell their tale direct ; the simple walks going where they are wanted ; flowers not set in patterns ; the walls and porch alive with flowers. Can the gentleman's garden then, too, be a picture? Certainly ; the greater the breadth and means the better the picture should be. But never if our formal "decorative" style of design is kept to. Reform must come by letting Nature take her just place in the garden.

Group of trees on garden lawn at Golder's Hill, Hampstead; picturesque effect in suburban garden

Natural and False Lines

After we have settled the essential approaches, levels, and enclosures for shelter, privacy, or dividing lines around a house, the natural form or lines of the earth herself are in nearly all cases the best to follow, and in my work I face any labour to get the ground back into its natural level or fall where disfigured by ugly banks, lines, or angles.

In the true Italian garden on the hills we have to alter the natural line of the earth or "terrace" it, because we cannot otherwise cultivate the ground or move at ease upon it. Such steep ground exists in many countries, and where it does, a like plan must be followed. The strictly formal in such ground is as right in its way as the lawn in a garden in the Thames valley. But the lawn is the heart of the true English garden, and as essential as the terrace is to the gardens on the steep hills. English lawns have too often been destroyed that " geometrical " gardens may be made where they are not only needless, but harmful both to the garden and home landscape. Sometimes on level ground the terrace walls cut off the view of the landscape from the house, and, on the other hand, the house from the landscape!

I hold that it is possible to get every charm of a garden and every use of a country-seat without sacrifice of the picturesque or beautiful; that there is no reason why, either in the working or design of gardens, there should be a single false line in them. By this I mean hard and ugly lines such as the earth never follows, as say, to mention a place known

Wakehurst. Elizabethan house, with grounds not terraced

to many, the banks about the head of the lake in the Bois de Boulogne. These lines are seen in all bad landscape work, though with good workmen I find it is as easy to form true and artistic lines as false and ugly ones. Every landscape painter or observer of landscape will know what is meant here, though I fear it is far beyond the limits of the ideas of design held by the authors of the *Formal Garden*. Also, that every charm of the flower garden may be secured by avoiding wholly the knots and scrolls which make all the plants and flowers of a garden, all its joy and life, subordinate to the wretched conventional design in which they are "set out." The true way is the opposite. We should see the flowers and feel the beauty of plant forms, with only the simplest possible plans to ensure good working, to secure every scrap of turf wanted for play or lawn, and for every enjoyment of a garden.

"Uncultivated Nature"

Such views I have urged, and carry them out when I can, in the hope of bringing gardening into a line with art, from which it is now so often divorced. It is natural that these views should meet with some opposition, and the consideration of the *Formal Garden* gives the opportunity of examining their value.

> The question, briefly stated, is this: Are we, in laying out our gardens, to ignore the house, and to reproduce uncultivated Nature to the best of our ability in the garden? Or are we to treat the house and garden as inseparable factors in one homogeneous whole, which are to co-operate for one premeditated result?

No sane person has ever proposed to ignore the house. So far from ignoring the house in my own work, where there is a beautiful house it tells me what to do! Unhappily, the house is often so bad that nothing can prevent its evil effect on the garden. "*Reproducing uncultivated Nature*" is no part of good gardening, as the whole reason of a flower garden is that it is a home for cultivated Nature. It is the special charm of the garden that we may have beautiful natural objects in their living beauty in it, but we cannot do this without care and culture to begin with! Whether it be Atlas Cedar or Eastern Cypress, Lily-tree or American Mountain Laurel, all must be cared for at first, and we must know their ways of life and growth if we are to treat them so that they will both grow well and be rightly placed—an essential point. And the more precious and rare they are the better the place they should have in the flower garden proper or pleasure ground, — places always the object of a certain essential amount of care even under the simplest and wisest plans. If we wish to encourage "uncultivated Nature" it must surely be a little further afield! A wretched flowerless pinched bedding plant and a great yellow climbing Tea Rose are both cultivated things, but what a vast difference in their beauty! There are many kinds of "cultivated Nature," and every degree of ugliness among them.

> Sir C. Barry's idea was that the garden was gradually to become less and less formal till it melted away into the park. Compromises such as these, however, will be rejected by thoroughgoing adherents of the formal gardens who hold that the garden should be avowedly separated from the adjacent country by a clean boundary line, a good high wall for choice. (*The Formal Garden.*)

Would any one put this high wall in front of Gilbert White's house at Selborne, or of Golder's Hill at Hampstead, or many English houses where

Gilbert White's house at Selborne. Example of many gardens with lawn coming to windows and flowers on its margin

the erection of a high wall would cut off the landscape? Not a word about the vast variety of such situations, each of which would require to be treated in a way quite different from the rest! There are many places in every county that would be robbed of their best charms by separating the garden from the adjacent country by a " good high wall."

> The custom of planting avenues and cutting straight lines through the woods surrounding the house to radiate in all directions was a departure from that strictly logical system which separated the garden from the park, and left the latter to take care of itself, a system which frankly subordinated Nature to art within the garden wall, but in return gave Nature an absolutely free hand outside it. (*The Formal Garden.*)

Nature an "*absolutely free hand*"! Imagine a great park or any part of an estate being left to Nature with an "absolutely free hand"! If it were, in a generation there would be very little to see but the edge of the wood. Callous to the beauty of English parks, he does not know that they are the object of much care, and he abuses all those who ever formed them, Brown, Repton, and the rest.

Example of formal gardening, with clipped trees and clipped shrubs in costly tubs

The True Landscape

Mr. Blomfield writes nonsense, and then attributes it to me—

> that is to say, we go to Claude, and having saturated our minds with his rocks and trees, we return to Nature and try to worry her into a resemblance to Claude.

I am never concerned with Claude, but seek the best expression I can secure of our beautiful English real landscapes, which are far finer than Claude's. At least I never saw any painted landscape like them—say that from the Chestnut Walk at Shrubland, looking over the lovely Suffolk country. That is the precious heritage we have to keep. And that is where simple and picturesque gardening will help us by making the garden a beautiful foreground for the true landscape, instead of cutting it off with a "high wall" or anything else that is ugly and needless.

> The lawns are not to be left in broad expanse, but to have Pampas Grasses, foreign shrubs, etc., dotted about on the surface.

I have fought for years against the lawn-destruction by the terrace-builders and bedding-out gardeners! But how are we to have our lawns in "broad expanse" if we build a high wall near the house to cut off even the possibility of a lawn? This has been done in too many cases to the ruin of all good effect and repose, often to shut out as good landscapes as ever were painted! There are flagrant cases in point to be found in private gardens in the suburbs of London. There is much bad and ignorant landscape work as there is bad building everywhere, but errors in that way are more easily removed than mistakes in costly and aimless work in brick and stone. At Coombe Cottage, when I first saw its useless terrace wall shutting out the beautiful valley view from the living rooms, I spoke of the error that had been made, but the owner thought that, as it had cost him a thousand pounds, he had better leave it where it was!

Buildings in Relation to the Garden

The place of formal gardening is clear for ever. The architect can help the gardener much by building a beautiful house! That is his work. The true architect, it seems to me, would seek to go no farther. The better the real work of the architect is done, the better for the garden and landscape. If there are any difficulties of level about the house beautiful, they should be dealt with by the architect, and the better his work and the necessary terracing, if any, are done, the pleasanter the work of the landscape or other gardener who has to follow him should be.

Longleat. Type of nobler English country seat with old house and picturesque planting

That a garden is made for plants is what most people who care for gardens suppose. If a garden has any use, it is to treasure for us beautiful flowers, shrubs, and trees. In these days—when our ways of building are the laughing-stock of all who care for beautiful buildings—there is plenty for the architect to do without spoiling our gardens! Most of the houses built in our time are so bad, that even the best gardening could hardly save them from contempt. Our garden flora is now so large, that a life's work is almost necessary to know it. How is a man to make gardens wisely if he does not know what has to be grown in them? I do not mean that we are to exclude other men than the landscape gardener proper from the garden. We want all the help we can get from those whose tastes and training enable them to help us—the landscape painter best of all, if he cares for gardens and trees — the country gentleman, or any keen student and lover of Nature. The landscape gardener of the present day is not always what we admire, his work often looking more like that of an engineer. His gardening near the house is usually a repetition of the decorative work of the house, of which I hope many artistic people are already tired. And as I think people will eventually see the evil and the wastefulness of this "decorative" stuff, and spend their money on really beautiful and artistic things, so I think the same often-repeated "knots" and frivolous patterns must leave the artistic garden, and simpler and dignified forms take their place.

To endeavour to apply any one preconceived plan or general idea to every site is folly, and the source of many blunders. The authors are not blind to the absurdities of the

Old Place, Lindfield. Picturesque garden of old English house, admitting of charming variety in its vegetation.

architectural gardeners, and say, on page 232 :—

> Rows of statues were introduced from the French, costly architecture superseded the simple terrace, intricate parterres were laid out from gardeners' pattern books, and meanwhile the flowers were forgotten. It was well that all this pomp should be swept away. We do not want this extravagant statuary, these absurdities in clipped work, this aggressive prodigality. But though one would admit that in its decay the formal garden became unmanageable and absurd, the abuse is no argument against the use.

Certainly not where the place calls for it, and all absolutely necessary stonework about a house should be controlled by the architect; beyond that, nothing. To let him lay out our home landscapes again with lines of trees, as shown in the old Dutch books, and with no regard to landscape design and to the relations of the garden to the surrounding country, would be the greatest evil that could come to the beautiful home landscapes of Britain.

Time and Gardens

Not one word of the swift worker, Time! Its effect on gardens is one of the first considerations. Fortress-town, castle, and moat all without further use! In old days gardens had to be set within the walls; hence, formal in outline, though often charming inside. To keep all that remains of such should be our first care; never to imitate them now! Many old gardens of this sort that remain to us are far more beautiful than the modern formal gardening, which by a strange perversity has been kept naked of plants or flower life! When safety came from civil war, then came to us the often beautiful Eliza-

bethan house, free of all moat or trace of war. At one time it was rash to make a garden away from the protecting walls. Now, any day in a country place beautiful situations may be found for certain kinds of gardens far away from the house, out of sight of it often.

Again, in the home fighting days there was less art away from the home. Rugged wastes and hills ; vast woodland districts near London ; even small houses moated to keep the cattle from wolves— fear of the rough hills and woods ! In those days an extension of the decorative work of the house into the garden had some novelty to carry it off, while the kinds of cultivated trees and shrubs were few. Hence if the old gardeners wanted an evergreen line, hedge, or bush of a certain height, they clipped an evergreen tree into the size they wanted. Notwithstanding this we have no evidence that anything like the geometrical monotony often seen in our own time existed then. To-day the ever-growing city, pushing its hard face over the once beautiful land, should make us wish more and more to keep such beauty of the earth as may be still possible to us. The horror of railway embankments, where were once the beautiful suburbs of London, cries to us to save all we can save of the natural beauty of the earth.

True Use of a Garden

It is surely flying in the face of Nature to fill our gardens with tropical plants, as we are urged to do by the writers on landscape gardening, ignoring the entire difference of climate and the fact that a colour which may look superb in the midst of other strong colours will look gaudy and vulgar amongst our sober tints, and that a leaf like that of the Yucca, which may be all very well in its own country, *is out of scale and character* amidst the modest foliage of our English trees. (*The Formal Garden.*)

A passage full of nonsense! The true use and first reason of a garden is to keep and grow for us plants *not* in our woods and mostly from other countries than our own! The Yucca, we are told by the authors, is a " plant out of scale and character among the modest foliage of our English trees "! The

Yuccas of our gardens are natives of the often cold plains of Eastern America, hardy in, and in every way fitted for, English gardens, but *not* amidst English trees. Is the aim of the flower-garden to show the " modest foliage " of English trees when almost every country house is surrounded by our native woods? According to such childish views, the noble Cedars in the park at Goodwood and on the lawn at Pain's Hill are out of place there! What is declared by Mr. Blomfield to be absurd is the soul of true gardening—to show, on a small scale it may be, some of the precious and inexhaustible loveliness of vegetation on plain or wood or mountain. This is the necessary and absolutely only true, just and fair use of a garden!

West Dean. Example of country seat in which terracing is needless, and in which turf may and indeed must often come

Formal Gardening

The very name of the book is a mistake. " Formal gardening " is rightly applied only to the gardens in which both the design and planting were formal and stupidly formal like the upper terrace of the Crystal Palace, Kensington Gore, as laid out by Nesfield, Crewe Hall ; and Shrubland, as laid out by Barry, in which, as in others of these architects' gardens, strict orders were given that no plants were to be allowed on the walls. The architect was so proud of his design, that he did not want the gardener at all, except to pound up bricks to take the place of flower colour ! It may be necessary to explain to some that this pounded brick and tile in lieu of colours has frequently been laid down in flower-gardens in our own day. To old gardens like Haddon and Rockingham, in which the vegetation about the house is perfectly free and natural in form, the term " formal gardening " is quite unfitted.

> But those who attack the old English formal garden do not take the trouble to understand its very considerable differences from the Continental gardens of the same period.

No one has "attacked" old English gardens. Part of my work has been to preserve much record of their beauty. The necessary terraces round houses like Haddon may be and are as beautiful as any garden ever made by man. Can anything be more unlike than the delicate veil of beautiful climbers and flowers over the grey walls of the courtyard at Ightham Mote and the walls of some gardens of our own day? The great

Athelhampton Hall, Dorset. Old English form with trees in their natural form.

dark rock-like feudal Berkeley is clad with Fig and Vine and Rose as far as they can reach. No trace in these old gardens of the modern " landscape architect," who said, My walls are not made for plants, and for my beds I prefer coloured brick!

What, then, is the kind of " Formal Gardening " that is bad? It is the purely formal or stone garden made for its own sake, often without a shadow of excuse. The garden of the Crystal Palace in part ; the stone garden at the head of the Serpentine ; Versailles ; the Grand Trianon ; Caserta, Schönbrunn are among the public gardens of Europe where this kind of garden is seen. Great harm has come to many a fair English lawn through this system. Let us learn by one instance, easily seen, the harm done in formal gardening, even where the ground called for an amount of terracing not usual in the plains and mostly gentle lawns of England—I mean the flower-garden at Shrubland Park, laid out by Sir Charles Barry, of which I have recently altered the plan and which I planted with graceful life where I found bare walls.

We will assume that the main terrace lines here are right, as the place stands on a bluff, and speak of a secondary evil of this formal gardening, which arose, I think, about the time Barry laid out Shrubland. That was that the walls of the house or garden were *not* to be graced by plants, and that to secure the keeping of the design, coloured gravels were to take the place of flowers. This rule, as is well known, has been carried out in many gardens—it was rigid here. I see it in some of the new gardens, and in asking at Worth Park why a long terra-cotta wall had not climbers on it, was told the designer would not allow it!

Yet Nature clothes the rock walls with beautiful life, even to the snow line, where the gems of the flower world stain the rocks with loveliest flowers. The crag walls of every alpine valley are her gardens; the Harebells toss their azure bells from the seams of the stones in the bridges across the mountain streams; the ruins of the temples of the great peoples of old, who really could build nobly, grow many a wild flower. Even when we take the stone and build with it, tender colours of lowly plants soon come and clothe the stone.

But the maker of these miserable garden walls, without use or need, says in effect, *Here Nature shall not come to hide my cleverness. I have built walls, and bare they must be!*

Well, with this bareness of the wall there were the usual geometrical pattern beds, many filled with sand and broken stone, and only very low and formal beds of flowers pinched into very low carpets, with much Box often edging beds a foot across. When I first went one spring day with Mr. Saumarez, we saw a large showy bed, and on going near, found it composed of pieces of broken brick painted yellow, blue, and red!

So, apart from needless formality of design and bare walls where no walls were wanted, there was often an ugly formality of detail, a senseless attempt to leave Nature out of the garden, an outrage against all that ever has or ever can make a garden delightful throughout the year by ruling that even the walls of the house should not shelter a Rose! And that is only part of what we get by letting "builders and decorators" waste precious means in stone that should be devoted to the living treasures of garden, lawn, or wood.

The Vicarage Garden, Oldham. One of numerous British gardens in which the conditions here declared to be essential are absent

"Nature" and what we mean by it

As to a natural school of landscape gardening, the authors say:

> A great deal is said about Nature and her beauty, and fidelity to Nature, and so on; but as the landscape gardener never takes the trouble to state precisely what he means by Nature, and, indeed, prefers to use the word in half a dozen different senses, we are not very much the wiser so far as principles are concerned.

They make this statement as if all beautiful natural landscape were a closed book; as if there were no stately Yews, in natural forms, on the Merrow Downs, as well as clipped Yews at Elvaston; as if the tree-fringed mountain lawns of Switzerland did not exist; or lovely evergreen glades on the Californian mountains, or wild Azalea gardens on those of Carolina, or even naturally-grown Planes in London squares.

There are many gardens and parks which clearly show what is meant by the "natural" style; and though, like others, this art is too often imperfect, we have so many instances of its success, that it is curious to find any one shutting his eyes to them. There are lessons in picturesque gardening in every country in Europe and in many parts of North America. Mr. Olmstead's work in America and Mr. Robert Marnock's in England teach them; they may be learnt in many English gardens—from Sir Richard Owen's little garden in Richmond Park to Dunkeld — even small rectory and cottage gardens, wholly free of architectural aids, show the principle. It was but a few weeks ago, in the garden of the English Embassy in

Paris, that I was struck with the simplicity of the lawn and plan of the garden there, and its fitness for a house in a city.

To support their idea that there is and can be no natural school of landscape gardening, the authors suppose what does not exist, and describe

> A piece of ground laid out with a studied avoidance of all order, all balance, all definite lines, and the result a hopeless disagreement between the house and its surroundings. This very effect can be seen in the efforts of the landscape gardener, and in old country houses, such as Barrington Court, near Langport, where the gardens have not been kept up.

Here, instead of taking one of the many good examples in Britain, they take poor, beautiful old Barrington, now an ill-kept farmhouse, with manure piled against the walls and the ceiling of the dining-room propped up with a Fir pole! The foolish proposition here laid down, that, because a garden is picturesque there must necessarily be a "*studied avoidance of all order, all balance, all definite lines,*" is disproved by hundreds of gardens in England. Why did not the authors take Miss Alice de Rothschild's garden at Eythorpe, or any beautiful and picturesque English garden, to compare with their results in stone and clipped and aligned trees?

Unclipped trees at the Little Trianon. (Compare with cut on p. 52.)

"All our Paths" are Crooked!

> For instance, because Nature is assumed never to show straight lines, all paths are to be made crooked ; because in a virgin forest there are no paths at all, let us in our acre and a half of garden make as little of the paths as possible. Deception is a primary object of the landscape gardener. (*The Formal Garden*.)

This, too, in the face of the facts of the case, of proof ready for the authors, in gardens in every country, from Prospect Park at Brooklyn to the English park at Munich. The fact that the Phœnix Park at Dublin is laid out in a fine, picturesque way does not forbid a great straight road through it—a road finer than in any strait-laced park in France. The late Robert Marnock was the best landscape gardener I have known, and I never saw one of his many gardens where he did not make an ample straight walk where an ample straight walk was required—as, indeed, many may remember is the case in the Botanic Gardens in the Regent's Park, laid out by him.

> Again, Nature is said to prefer a curved line to a straight, and it is thence inferred that all the lines in a garden, and especially paths, should be curved.
>
> The utter contempt for design of the landscape gardener is shown most conspicuously in his treatment of paths. He lays them about at random, and keeps them so narrow that they look like threads, and there is barely room to walk abreast.

The opposite of this is indeed the truth, for many gardens and parks laid out with some regard to landscape beauty are partly spoiled by the size and number of the walks, as in the gardens around Paris—the Parc Monceau and Buttes Chaumont, for instance. The slightest

Westonbirt

knowledge of gardens would show that walks like threads are no necessary part of landscape gardening!

This error shows well the effect of men reading and writing about what they have not seen.

The axiom on which landscape gardening rests is declared by Messrs. Blomfield and Thomas to be

Whatever Nature does is right; therefore let us go and copy her (p. 5).

Here is a poor sneer at true art, not only at art in landscape gardening, but in all the fine arts. The central and essential idea of the landscape art is choice of what is beautiful—not taking the salt waste in Utah, or a field of weeds, or a Welsh slope of decayed slate, or the bog of Allen, or the thousand other things in Nature that are monotonous or dull to us, even though here and there beautiful as a wide bog may be. We can have in a garden a group of Scotch Firs as good in form as a fine group in wild Nature, and so of the Cedar of Lebanon and many of the lovely trees of the world. We can have bits of rock alive with alpine flowers, or pieces of lawn fringed with trees in their natural forms and as graceful as the alpine lawns on the Jura.

So of all other true art. The Venus of Milo is from a noble type of woman —not a mean Greek. The horses of the Parthenon are the best types of Eastern breed, full of life and beauty, not sickly beasts. Great landscape painters like Corot, Turner, and Troyon show us in their work the absurdity of this statement so impertinently used. They seek not ugly things because they are natural, but beautiful combinations of field, and hill, wood, water, tree, and flower, and grass, selecting groupings which go to make good composition, and then waiting for the most beautiful effects of morning, evening, or whatever light suits the chosen subject best, so give us lovely pictures! But they work always from faithful study of Nature and from stores of knowledge gathered from Nature study, and that is the only true path for the landscape gardener; as all true and great art can only be based on the eternal laws of Nature.

"The Only Garden Possible!"

The word "garden" itself means an enclosed space, a garth or yard surrounded by walls, as opposed to unenclosed fields and woods. The formal garden, with its insistence on strong bounding lines, is, strictly speaking, the only "garden" possible.

All other gardens are, of course, impossible to the authors — the Parc Monceau, the informal gardens about Paris, Glasnevin, the Botanic Gardens in Regent's Park and at Sheffield, Golder's Hill, Greenlands, Pendell Court, Rhianva, and the thousand cottage, rectory, and other British gardens where no wall is seen! The Bamboo garden at Shrubland, the Primrose garden at Munstead, the rock and other gardens,

Thrumpton Hall. A type of numerous English gardens with informal planting

which we must keep in quiet places away from any sight of walls, are all "*impossible*" to these authors! How much better it would be for every art if it were impossible for men to write about things of which by their own showing they have not even elementary knowledge!

And the sketches in the book show us what these possible gardens are! They are careful architects' drawings, deficient in light and shade ; not engraved, but reproduced by a hard process, some being mere reproductions of old engravings ; and diagrams of old " knots " and " patterns," with birds and ships perched on wooden trellises, without the slightest reference to any human or modern use. A curious one of Badminton will show fully the kind of plan the authors wish to see revived. Some of the illustrations show the evils of the system which the authors advocate, notably one of Levens Hall, Westmoreland, a very interesting and real old garden. Interesting as it is from age, the ugliness of the clipped forms takes away from the beauty of the house. Even in sketches of gardens like Montacute and Brympton, the beauty of the gardens is not well shown. The most interesting drawings, it is not surprising to find, are the informal ones! Many of the others show the *evil*, not the good, of the system advocated, by their hard lines and the emphasising of ugly forms.

"No Design in Landscape"

> Horticulture stands to garden design much as building does to architecture. This book has been written entirely from the standpoint of the designer, and therefore contains little or no reference to the actual methods of horticulture.

Throughout the book it is modestly assumed that there can be no "design" in anything but in lines of stone, and clipped trees to "harmonise" with the stone, and to bring in "order" and "balance." A Longleat, Highclere or Little Trianon, or any of the many English places which are planted in picturesque ways can show no design; but a French town, with its wretched lines of tortured Limes, is "pure" and "broad" in design. The *naïveté* of the book in this respect is often droll. One amusing passage is on p. 54 :—

> However rich the details, there is no difficulty in grasping the principle of a *garden laid out in an equal number of rectangular plots.* Everything is straightforward and logical ; you are not bored with hopeless attempts to master the bearings of the garden.

This is the kitchen gardener's view, and that of the market gardener of all countries, but the fun is in calling the idea of it "*grasping a principle*"! At this rate makers of chessboards have strong claims to artistic merit !

No wonder that men who call a "principle" the common way of setting out kitchen and cabbage gardens from Pekin to Mortlake can see no design in the many things that go to make a beautiful landscape !

Equally stupid is the assumption, throughout the book, that the people the authors are pleased to term "landscapists" flop their houses down in the

Grass, and never use low walls for dividing lines, nor terraces where necessary, never use walls for shelter or privacy, have no " order " or " balance," and presumably allow the Nettles to look in at the windows, and the cattle to have a fine time with the Carnations!

No Grass in Landscape Gardening!

The following glaring piece of injustice is due to want of the most elementary consideration of garden design :—

> Grass-work as an artistic quantity can hardly be said to exist in landscape gardening. It is there considered simply as so much background to be broken up with shrubs and Pampas Grass and irregular beds (p. 135).

The opposite of this is the fact. Grass-work as an "artistic quantity" did not exist in anything like the same degree before landscape gardening. One of the faults of the formal style of gardening still seen in France and Austria is that there is little or no Grass. Compare the Jardin des Plantes in Paris with the Parc

Goodwood. Example of large English places in which the grass sweeps up to the house

Monceau, or the many other gardens about Paris in which Grass is an "artistic quantity." One of the most effective reasons indeed for adopting the English landscape garden was that it gave people some fresh and open Grass, often with picturesque surroundings, and, nowadays, one can hardly travel on the continent and not see some pleasant results of this. In England, the landscape gardeners and writers have almost destroyed every trace of the stiff old formal gardens, and we cannot judge the ill effects of the builder's garden so easily as in France. As a rule, the want of rest and freshness in tropical and sub-tropical gardens is due to the absence of those broad and airy breadths of greensward which, in gardens at least, are largely due to landscape gardening. Think of Warwick without its turf and glorious untrimmed Cedars!

Consider the difference between a

picturesque landscape like the Emperor of Austria's stately garden at Laxenberg, near Vienna, and the gardens in the same city formed of miserable clipped trees in lines! Grass as an "artistic quantity" is finely visible at Laxenberg; in the old clipped gardens gravel and distorted trees are the only things seen in quantity —we cannot call it "artistic."

"Landscapist" is used throughout the book as a term of contempt. The authors take some of the worst work that is possible, and condemn all in the same opprobrious terms, as if we were to condemn the noble art of the builders of the Parthenon on seeing a "jerry" building in London. They may be quite sure that there *is* a true and beautiful art of landscape gardening, notwithstanding their denunciations, and it is none the less real because there is no smug definition of it that pleases the minds of men who declare that it does not exist.

GARDEN DESIGN 49

> The horticulturist and the gardener are indispensable, *but they should work under control*, and they stand in the same relation to the designer as the artist's colourman does to the painter, or, perhaps it would be fairer to say, as the builder and his workmen stand to the architect.

What modesty! The men whose business it is to design gardens are heartily abused. How very graceful it would be on the part of one of them to write an essay telling architects how to build, and showing that to build well it is not necessary to know anything about the inhabitants or uses of a house!

"Improving" Battersea Park!

Perhaps after the cemetery, the ugliest things in the fair land of France are the ugly old lines of clipped Limes which deface many French towns. Readers who have not seen these things can have no idea of their abominable hardness and ugliness, the natural form of the trees being destroyed, and deformed and hideous trees resulting from constant clipping. These gouty lines of clipped trees are praised as " noble walls " " pure and broad " in design, while

> Such a place, for instance, as Battersea Park is like a bad piece of architecture, full of details which stultify each other. The only good point in it is the one avenue, and this leads to nowhere.

Avenue in Paris. Shewing that even in a land of clipped trees clipping is not essential

If this park had been planted out with groves and avenues of Limes, like the boulevard at Avallon, or the squares at Vernon, or even like the east side of Hyde Park between the Achilles statue and the Marble Arch, at least one definite effect would have been reached. There might have been shady walks, and noble walls of trees, instead of the spasmodic futility of Battersea Park.

Battersea Park, like many others, may be capable of improvement; but here we have men who want to supplant its lawns, grassy playgrounds, and pretty retired gardens with Lime trees like those of a French town, and lines and squares of trees like those at Vernon, which I once saw half bare of leaves long before the summer was over!

The authors see with regret that the good sense of planters has for many years been gradually emancipated from the style (as old as the Romans and older) of planting in rows. It was the very early and in a very real sense a barbarous way. Since the days when country places were laid out "in a number of rectangular plots," whole worlds of lovely things have come to us—to give one instance only, the trees of California, Oregon, and the Rocky Mountains. For men to talk of designing homes for such things, who say they have no knowledge of them, is absurdity itself!

Clipped trees at the Little Trianon

"*An unerring perception told the Greeks that the beautiful must also be the true, and recalled them back into the way. As in conduct they insisted on an energy which was rational, so in art and in literature they required of beauty that it, too, should be before all things rational."*—PROFESSOR BUTCHER, in *Some Aspects of the Greek Genius*.

NATURE AND CLIPPED YEWS

The remarks quoted below on Nature and the clipping shears are not from Josh Billings, but from *The Formal Garden*, of which the literary merit, we are told in the preface, belongs to Mr. Blomfield.

> A clipped Yew tree is as much a part of Nature —that is, subject to natural laws—as a forest Oak ; but the landscapist, by appealing to associations which surround the personification of Nature, holds up the clipped Yew tree to obloquy as something against Nature. So far as that goes, it is no more unnatural to clip a Yew tree than to cut Grass.

I believe we cut Grass when we want hay, or soft turf to play on, but disfiguring a noble tree is not a necessary part of our work either for our profit or pleasure. Perhaps, as is probable, Mr. Blomfield has never noticed what a beautiful tree a Yew in its natural form is. It is not only on the hills he may see them. If he will come and see them in my own garden in a high wind some day, or when bronzed a little with a hard winter, he may change his amusing notions about clipped Yews.

I think I can give Mr. Blomfield a rational explanation of why it is foolish to clip so fair a tree or any *tree*.

I clip Yews when I want to make a hedge of them, but then I am clipping a hedge, and not a tree. I hold up " the clipped Yew tree to obloquy," as the tree in its natural form is the most beautiful evergreen tree of our western world—as fine as the Cedar in its plumy branches, and more beautiful than any Cedar in the colour of its stem. In our own day we have seen trees of the same

The "Grange," Hartley Wintney

great order as the Yew gathered from a thousand hills—from British Columbia, through North America and Europe to the Atlas Mountains, and not one of them has yet proved to be so beautiful as our native Yew when it is allowed to grow unclipped root or branch. But in gardens the quest for the strange and exotic is so constant, that few give a fair chance to the Yew as a tree, while in graveyards where it is so often seen in a very old state, the frequent destruction of the roots in grave-digging prevents the tree from reaching its full stature and beauty, though there are Yews in English churchyards that have lived through a thousand winters.

I do not clip my Yews, because clipping destroys the shape of one of the most delightful in form of all trees, beautiful, too, in its plumy branching. It is not my own idea only that I urge here, but that of all who have ever thought of form, foremost among whom we must place artists who have the happiness of always drawing natural forms. Let Mr. Blomfield stand near one of the Cedar-like Yews by the Pilgrim's Way on the North Downs, and, comparing it with trees cut in the shape of an extinguisher, consider what the difference means to the artist who seeks beauty of form. Clipping such trees does not merely deserve " obloquy " ; it is worse than idiotic, as there is a sad reason for the idiot's ways.

If I use what in the Surrey nurseries are called " hedging Yews " to form a hedge, high or low, I must clip them to form my hedge, and go on doing so if I wish to keep it, or the hedge would soon show me that it was " subject to natural laws," and escape from the shears.

What right have we to deform things given us so perfect and lovely in form ? No cramming of Chinese feet into im-

possible shoes is half so wicked as the wilful distortion of the divinely beautiful forms of trees. The cost of this hideous distortion alone is one reason against it, as one may soon find out in places where miles of trees cut into wall-like shape have to be clipped, as at Versailles and Schönbrunn! This clipping is a mere survival of the day when gardens had very few trees, and it was necessary to clip the few they had to fit certain situations to conform to the architect's notion of " garden design." This is not design at all from any landscape point of view; and though the elements which go to form beautiful landscape, whether home landscape or the often higher landscape beauty of the open country, are often subtle, and though they are infinitely varied, they are none the less real. The fact that men when we had few trees clipped them into walls and grotesque shapes to make them serve their notions of " design " is surely not a reason why we, who have the trees of a thousand hills with trees of almost every size and shape among them, should violate and mutilate some of the finest natural forms!

Thus while it may be right to clip a tree to form a wall, dividing-line, or hedge, it is never so to clip trees grown as single specimens or groups, as by clipping such we only get ugly forms—unnatural, too. Last autumn, in Hyde Park, I saw a man clipping Hollies at the Rotten Row end of the Serpentine, and asking him why it was done, he said it was to "keep them in shape," though, to do him justice, he added that he thought it would be better to let them alone. Men who clip so handsome a tree as the Holly when taking no part in a hedge or formal line are blind to beauty of form. To tolerate such clipped forms is to prove oneself

Building in Paris. Showing that intimate association with buildings does not necessitate clipping or distortion of trees

callous to natural beauty of tree form, and to show that we cannot even see ugliness.

Take, again, the clipped Laurels by which many gardens and drives are disfigured. Laurel in its natural shape in the woods of west country or other places, where it is let alone, is often fine in form, though we may have too much of it. But it is planted everywhere without thought of its stature or fitness for the spot, and then it grows until the shears are called in, and we see nearly every day its fine leaves and free shoots cut short back into ugly banks and sharp, wall-like, or formless masses, disfiguring many gardens without the slightest necessity. There is no place in which it is used clipped for which we could not get shrubs quite suitable that would not need mutilation. It is not only clipped trees that are ugly, but even trees like the Irish Yew, Wellingtonia, and some Arbor-vitæ, which frequently assume shapes like extinguishers or the forms of clipped trees. It often happens that these, when over-planted or planted near houses, so emphasise ugly forms about the house, that there is no beauty possible in the home landscape. Many of such ugly, formless trees have been planted within the last generation, greatly to the injury of the garden landscape.

In the old gardens, where, from other motives, trees were clipped when people had very few Evergreens or shrubs of any kind, or where they wanted an object of a certain height, they had to clip. It is well to preserve such gardens, but never to imitate them, as has been done in various English and American gardens. If we want shelter, we can get it in various delightful ways without clipping, and, while getting it, we can enjoy the beautiful natural forms of the finest

Evergreens. Hedges and wall-like dividing lines of green living things will now and then be useful, and even may be artistically used ; they are sometimes, however, used where a wall would be better, walls having the great advantage of not robbing the ground near. A wall is easily made into a beautiful garden with so many lovely things, too, from great scrambling yellow Roses to alpine flowers. To any one with the slightest sympathy with Nature or art these things need not be said.

No Line in Nature!

Now as a matter of fact in Nature—that is, in the visible phenomena of the earth's surface—there are no lines at all; "a line" is simply an abstraction which conveniently expresses the direction of a succession of objects which may be either straight or curved. "Nature" has nothing to do with either straight lines or curved; it is simply begging the question to lay it down as an axiom that curved lines are more "natural" than straight.

Then men must never again talk of the "lines" of a ship! Perhaps Mr. Blomfield would accept a plumb line? One can hardly leave London an hour before a person who looks at the landscape may see the lines or boundaries between one mass and another. Who could stand amongst downs or an alpine valley and say there are no lines in them, inasmuch as one of the most visible and delightful things in all such cases is the beauty of those lines? This is the key of the whole question of landscape gardening. There is no good landscape gardening possible without a feeling for the natural gradation and forms of the earth.

It can be seen in little things, like the slope of a field as well as in the slope of a mountain, and it is the neglect of this which leaves us so little to boast of in landscape work. In a country slightly diversified it is, of course, more important than in a perfectly flat one, but in all diversified ground no good landscape work can be done without regarding the natural gradation of the earth, which will often tell us what to do. It is blindness to this principle which makes so many people cut their roads and walks crudely through banks, leaving straight sharp sides—false lines, in fact—when a little care and observation would have avoided this and given a true and beautiful line for a road or walk.

Once the necessary levels are settled and the garden walks by straight walls about the house are got away from, we soon come to ground which, whether we treat it rightly or not, will at once show whether the work done be landscape work or not. No plan, it seems to me, is so good as keeping to the natural form of the earth in all lawn, pleasure ground, and plantation work. Roads, paths, fences, plantations, and anything like wood will be all the better if we are guided by natural lines or forms, taking advantage of every difference of level and every little accident of the ground for our dividing lines and other beginnings or endings.

In the absence of any guidance of

Broadlands, Hants

this sort, what we see is brutal cutting through banks, lines like railway embankments—without the justification there is for the sharpness of a railway embankment—and ugly banks to roads, very often ugly in their lines too. If we are ever to have a school of true landscape gardening, the study and observation of the true gradation of the earth must be its first task.

"Vegetable Sculpture"[1]

This gentleman, unfortunately without any knowledge of plants, trees, or landscape beauty, launches out into the dreary sea of quotations from old books about gardens, and knows so little of where he is going, that he is put out of his course by every little drift of wind.

One goes through chapter after chapter thinking to get to the end of the weary matter only to find again nothing but quotations, even to going back to an old book for a song. When at last we come to a chapter on "*Art in the*

[1] *Garden Craft, Old and New.* By John D. Sedding. London: Kegan Paul, Trench, Trübner and Co.

Warren House, Coombe Wood

Garden," this is what is offered us as sense on a charming subject, familiar to many, so that all may judge of the depth of this foolish talk about it! Such a writer discussing in this way a metaphysical or obscure subject might swim on in his inky water for ever, and no one know where he was!

> Let us here point to the fact, that any garden whatsoever is but Nature idealised, pastoral scenery rendered in a fanciful manner. It matters not what the date, size, or style of the garden, it represents an idealisation of Nature. *Real* nature exists outside the artist and apart from him. The Ideal is that which the artist conceives to be an interpretation of the outside objects, or that which he adds to the objects. The garden gives imaginative form to emotions the natural objects have awakened in man. The *raison d'être* of a garden is man's feeling the *ensemble*.

But we cannot allow him to bring the false and confusing "art" drivel of the day into the garden without showing the absurdity of his ideas.

The illustrations are of the most

wretched kind produced by some process, the only interesting one being one of Levens. The most childish ideas of the garden prevail—indeed we hardly like to call them childish, because children do put sensible questions and see clearly. For instance, for the author there is no art in gardening at all—the " art " consists entirely of building walls and planting Yew hedges. Thus the work of the late James Backhouse, who knew every flower on the hills of Northern England, and expressed that knowledge in his charming rock garden, is not art, but cutting a tree into the shape of a cocked hat *is* art, according to Mr. Sedding!

He assumes that landscape gardeners all follow artistic ways, and that only architects make terraces ; whereas the greatest sinners in this respect have been landscape gardeners—Nesfield and Paxton. He has paid so little attention

Drummond Castle. Example of beautiful garden in Scotland, in position requiring terracing

to the subject, that he says that the landscape gardener's only notion is to put Grass all around the house! It does not even occur to him that there may be Grass on one side of a house and gardens of various sorts at the others, as at Goodwood, Shrubland, Knole, and that a house may have at each side a different expression of landscape gardening!

He takes the *English Flower Garden* as the expression of landscape gardening practice; whereas the book, in all the parts that treat of design, is a protest against the formation by landscape gardeners of costly things which have nothing to do with gardening and nothing to do with true architecture. The good architect is satisfied with building a beautiful house, and that we are all the happier for. But what we have to deplore is that men who are not really architects, who are not gardeners, should cover the earth with rubbish like the Crystal Palace basins, the thing at the top of the Serpentine, and the Grand Trianon at Versailles.

Here is a specimen of Mr. Sedding's knowledge of the landscape art.

> For the "landscape style" does not countenance a straight line, or terrace, or architectural form, or symmetrical beds about the house, for to allow these would not be to photograph Nature. As carried into practice, the style demands that the house shall rise abruptly from the Grass, and the general surface of the ground shall be *characterised by smoothness and bareness (like Nature!)*.

If he had even taken the trouble to see a good garden laid out by Mr. Marnock or anybody worthy of the name of landscape gardener, he would find that they knew the use of the terrace very well. If he had taken the trouble to see one of my own gardens, he would find beds quite as formal, but not so frivolous as those described in the older books, and lines simple and straight

Madresfield. Example of modern English garden.

as they can be. Where Barry left room for a dozen flowers at Shrubland I put one hundred ; so much for the "*bareness*"!

On page 180 he says :—

> I have no more scruple in using the scissors upon tree or shrub, where trimness is desirable, than I have in mowing the turf of the lawn that once represented a virgin world. There is a quaint charm in the results of the topiary art, in the prim imagery of evergreens, that all ages have felt. And I would even introduce Bizarreries on the principle of not leaving all that is wild and odd to Nature outside of the garden paling ; and in the formal part of the garden *my Yews should take the shape of pyramids, or peacocks, or cocked hats, or ramping lions in Lincoln green, or any other conceit I had a mind to, which vegetable sculpture can take.*

After reading this I saw again some of the true " vegetable sculpture " that I have been fortunate to see ; Reed and Lily, a model for ever in stem, leaf, and bloom ; the grey Willows of Britain, sometimes lovelier than Olives against our skies ; many-columned Oak groves set in seas of Primroses, Cuckoo flowers and Violets; Silver Birch woods of Northern Europe beyond all grace possible in stone ; the eternal garland of beauty that one kind of Palm waves for hundreds of miles throughout the land of Egypt,—a vein of summer in a lifeless world : the noble Pine woods of California and Oregon, like fleets of colossal masts on mountain waves—saw again these and many other lovely forms in garden and woodland, and then wondered that any one could be so blind to the beauty of plant and tree as to write as Mr. Sedding does here.

From the days of the Greeks to our own time, the delight of all great artists has been to get as near this divine beauty as the material they work with permits. But this deplorable " *vegetable sculptor's* " delight is in distorting beautiful natural forms ; and this in the one art in which we enjoy the living things themselves, and not merely representations of them!

The old people from whom he takes his ideas were not nearly so foolish, as when the Yew tree was used as a shelter or a dividing line, and when a Yew was put at a garden door for shelter or to form a hedge, it was necessary to clip it if it was not to get out of all bounds. But here is a man delighting for its own sake in what he calls with such delicate feeling "*vegetable sculpture,*" in "cocked hats" and "ramping lions"!

www.ingramcontent.com/pod-product-compliance
Lightning Source LLC
Chambersburg PA
CBHW021940160426
43195CB00011B/1161